n my

THE BOOK

by Mario Garza

Copyright © 2006 by Mario Garza.
All rights reserved. No part of this book may be reproduced
in any form without written permission from the publisher.

Library of Congress Cataloging-in-Publication Data:
Garza, Mario, 1984-
  Stuff on my cat : the book / Mario Garza.
    p. cm.
  ISBN-10: 0-8118-5538-4
  ISBN-13: 978-0-8118-5538-9
  1. Photography, Humorous. 2. Photography of cats. I. Title.
  TR679.5.G37 2006
  636.8002'07—dc22

                                2005035256

Manufactured in China

Drawings by Deth P. Sun

Designed by Ayako Akazawa

Distributed in Canada by Raincoast Books
9050 Shaughnessy Street
Vancouver, British Columbia V6P 6E5

10 9 8 7 6 5 4 3 2 1

Chronicle Books LLC
85 Second Street
San Francisco, California 94105

www.chroniclebooks.com

INTRODUCTION

My cat, Love, has ruled over our household since the day she arrived as a feeble little kitten. We spent many quality hours together playing the string game. She was particularly fond of being chased around the house and pawing my ankles as I bustled by. Love was the cutest kitten you've ever seen, and it seems all she really needed in life was some attention and a bit of TLC.

Fast-forward eight years: We're waking up at 5 a.m. every morning because she's been meowing bloody murder in our ears for the past twenty minutes. We let her out to go do her business. One minute later, just as you manage to get comfortable again, she demands entrance back into the house. Love has also turned my laundry pile into her personal paradise. She lies there on her back, belly up, tongue halfway out, in deep sleep and purring like a rusty chainsaw. She likes to leave her white fur all over our dark clothes as a reminder of who runs the joint, too. I still love her, but what happened to the good old days? How can the two of us be best buds if she's always sleeping?

Then one day several years ago, it clicked. She was lying there on her back without a care in the world. I casually placed a Pez dispenser on her head and left to go about my business. I came back fifteen minutes later, and it was still there undisturbed. From then on, I knew exactly how we'd be spending time together. At first this little game started off small: quarters, pens, bottle caps, and keys. Soon we graduated to shoes, wallets, cameras, and cell phones. (Others didn't stop there: peer deeper into the book and you'll be pleasantly surprised at what some cat owners have managed to get away with.) The game became a regular occurrence in our house, and the objects grew larger and stranger.

While putting increasingly outrageous stuff on my cat, I've noticed a very satisfying shift of power going on. Love rules the house the majority of the time—she goes where she wants when she wants, she naps wherever she pleases, and the petting starts and ends at her command. But my, how times have changed. Now I'm in control when I sneak up behind her and place a pancake on top of her head—checkmate.

With all of the fun I was having putting stuff on my cat, I figured there must be other people out there doing the same thing. In July 2005 I decided that I would start an online community for these kindred spirits. Stuffonmycat.com was born and came with a simple and powerful message: **stuff + cats = awesome**. I snapped some pictures of my object-laden cat and posted them. Within just a couple of months, the site took off and became one of those weird online phenomena that no one can really explain. Millions of curious people visited, and thousands of them submitted pictures of their own cats with various things on them. As you'll see in this book, the quality and variety of the submissions was outstanding. Yahoo! and *GQ* magazine dubbed Stuffonmycat.com one of the coolest sites of the year.

Unfortunately, some cats aren't as tolerant as mine and need a bit of extra help to bring out their maximum stacking potential. For the owners of such cats, I offer a bit of advice: Before you try to put anything on your cat, make sure to get on his good side. Pet him until he reaches a euphoric state on the brink of a nap. When you're about to put something on your cat, be sure to try to make the process as quick and seamless as possible. If you pretend you do this all the time, kitty won't think much of it, but if you make a big deal out of it he may catch on to you. Try not to make a big commotion, and have this be a one-on-one game—too many people in the room may get kitty paranoid. Lastly, try to snap a picture as soon as you can. It would be a shame if you put all that effort into a nice stack and your cat decided to roll over.

Some people still don't *understand* the Stuff on My Cat philosophy, but most seem to embrace it. I have yet to find someone who can look through these photos with a straight face. Love and I see a lot more of each other nowadays, and the game just about saved our sagging relationship. If you want in on the action, just snap some pictures of stuff on your cat and send them over. I'd love to see them. But for now I have to get going—my cat is napping, and there's a slice of pizza with her name on it.

—Mario Garza

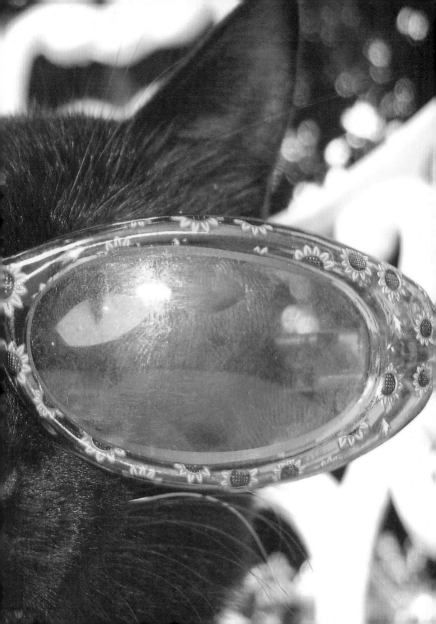

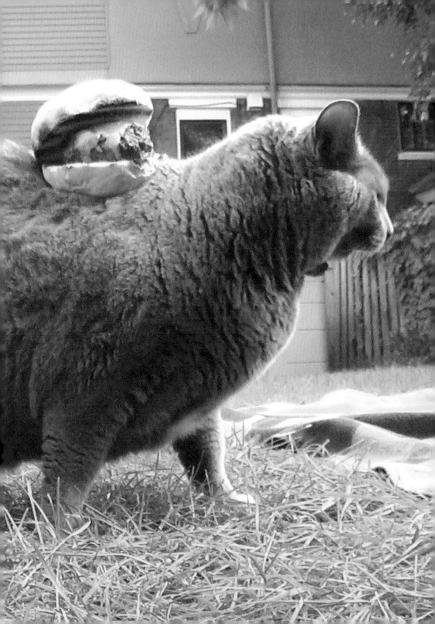

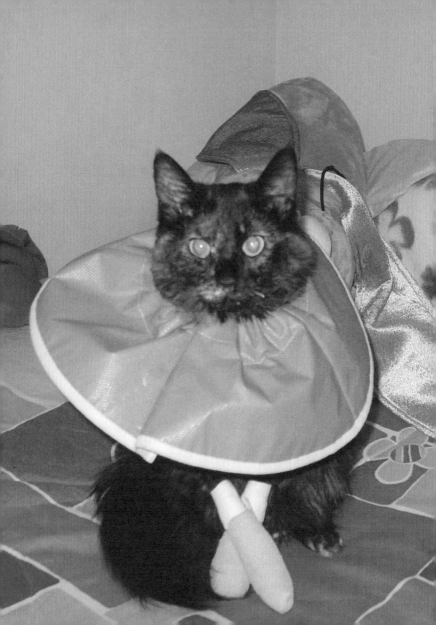

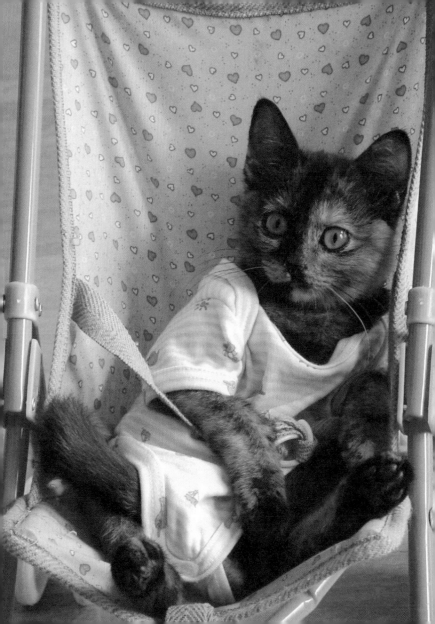

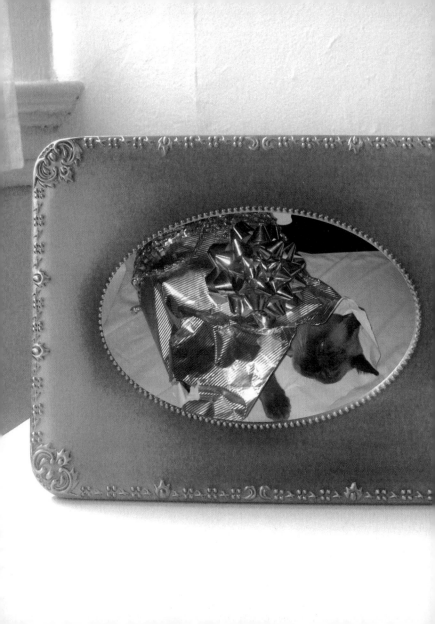

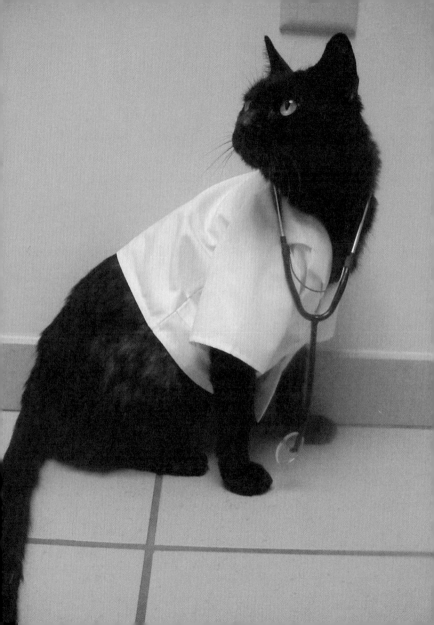

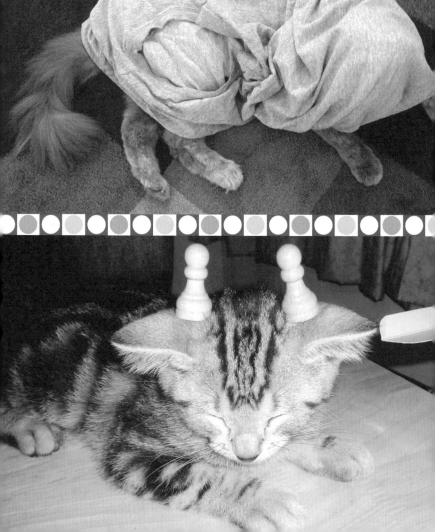

AMANDA

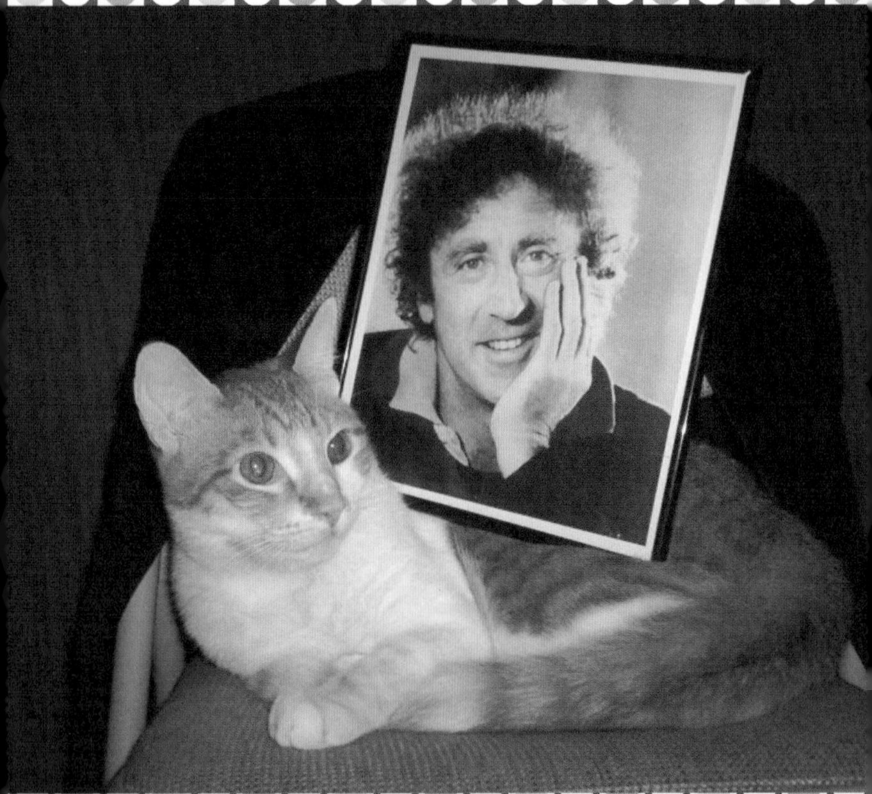

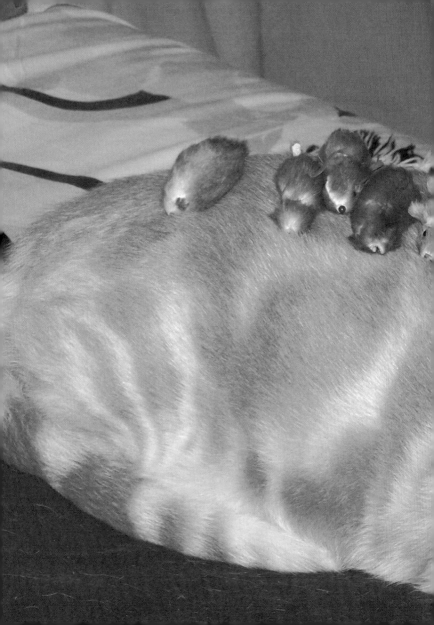

MARCY ♡
BENJAMIN

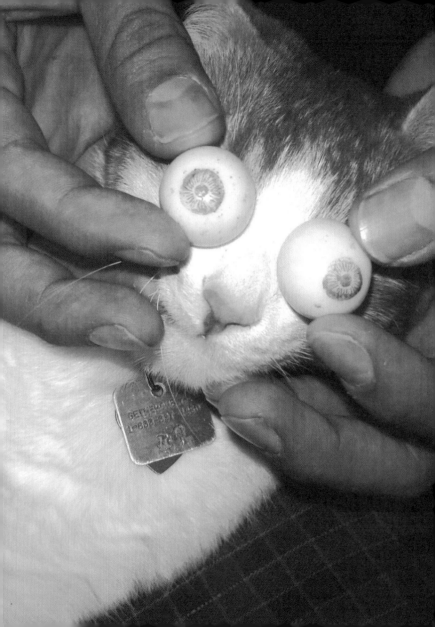

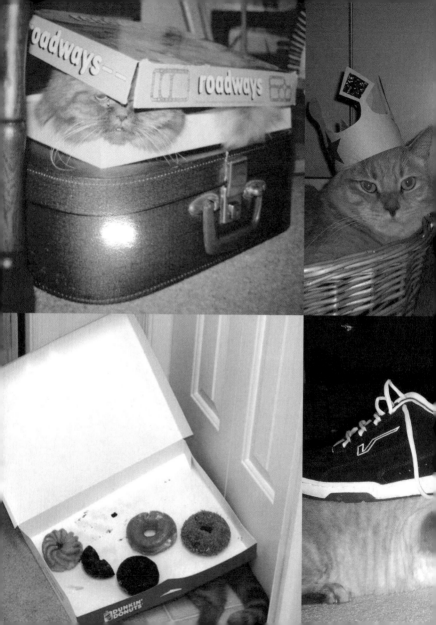

Mario Garza is a full-time student and freelance graphic designer. As a spur of the moment joke he launched Stuffonmycat.com. He and his cat, Love, live in Fresno, California.